D1545328

AFRICAN AMERICAN
POLITICIANS &
CIVIL RIGHTS ACTIVISTS

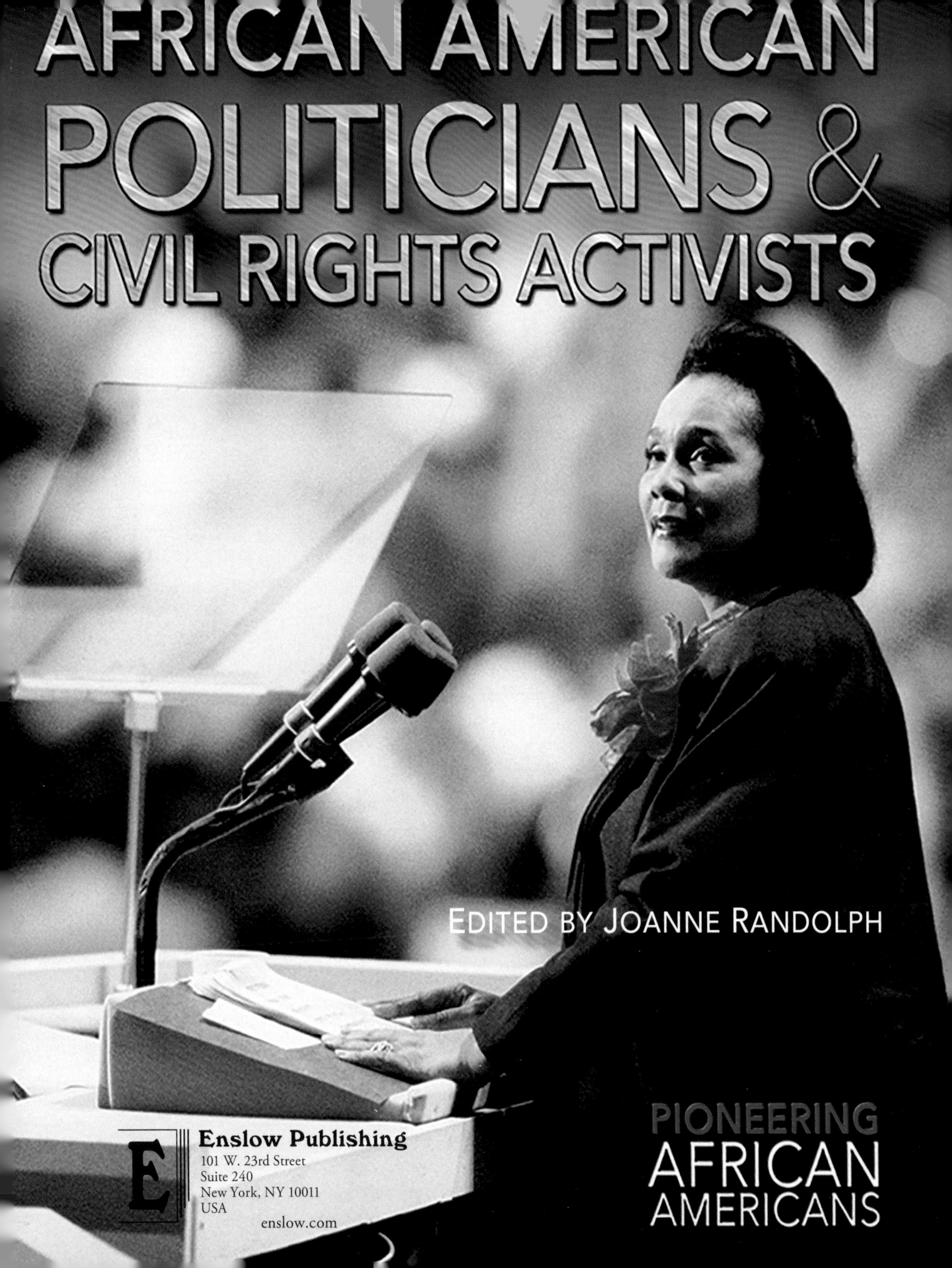

EDITED BY JOANNE RANDOLPH

Enslow Publishing
101 W. 23rd Street
Suite 240
New York, NY 10011
USA

enslow.com

PIONEERING
AFRICAN
AMERICANS

This edition published in 2018 by:
Enslow Publishing, LLC.
101 W. 23rd Street, Suite 240
New York, NY 10011

Library of Congress Cataloging-in-Publication Data

Names: Randolph, Joanne, editor.
Title: African American politicians & civil rights activists / edited by Joanne Randolph.
Description: New York, NY : Enslow Publishing, 2018. | Series: Pioneering African Americans | Includes bibliographical references and index. | Audience: Grades 5-8.
Identifiers: LCCN 2017021663| ISBN 9780766092525 (library bound) | ISBN 9780766093959 (pbk.) | ISBN 9780766093966 (6 pack)
Subjects: LCSH: African Americans—Civil rights—Juvenile literature. | African American civil rights workers—Biography—Juvenile literature. | African American politicians—Biography—Juvenile literature. | Civil rights movements—United States—Juvenile literature.
Classification: LCC E185.96 .A448 2018 | DDC 323.092/2 [B] —dc23
LC record available at https://lccn.loc.gov/2017021663

Printed in the United States of America

To Our Readers: We have done our best to make sure all website addresses in this book were active and appropriate when we went to press. However, the author and the publisher have no control over and assume no liability for the material available on those websites or on any websites they may link to. Any comments or suggestions can be sent by email to customerservice@enslow.com.

Photos Credits: Cover, pp. 3, 45 Wally McNamee/Corbis Historical/Getty Images; pp. 5, 7, 23, 30, 33 Bettmann/Getty Images; pp. 9, 12, 16, 21, 22 Library of Congress Prints and Photographs Division; pp. 11, 17 Stock Montage/Archive Photos/Getty Images; p. 14 Robert Parent/The LIFE Images Collection/Getty Images; p. 19 David Attie/Michael Ochs Archives/Getty Images; p. 26 Photo12/Universal Images Group/Getty Images; p. 28 Hulton Archive/Moviepix/Getty Images; p. 34 The George F. Landegger Collection of District of Columbia Photographs in Carol M. Highsmith's America, Library of Congress, Prints and Photographs Division; p. 36 Thomas D. Mcavoy/The LIFE Picture Collection/Getty Images; p. 40 Howard Sochurek/The LIFE Picture Collection/Getty Images; p. 43 CNP/Hulton Archive/Getty Images; interior pages Sebastian Duda//Shutterstock.com (gavel).

Article Credits: Christine Graf and Annabel Wildrick, "Sowing the Seeds for the Civil Rights Movement," *AppleSeeds*; Peter Roop, "Five Leaders for Freedom," *Cobblestone*; Meg Greene, "*The Crisis* Is Born," *Cobblestone*; Craig E. Blohm and Kathiann M. Kowalski, "Organizing for the Cause," *Cobblestone*; Leslie Anderson Morales, "Ida B. Wells-Barnett: The Later Years," *Cobblestone*; Eric Arnesen, "Charles Hamilton Houston: Learning from the Best," *Footsteps*; Jim Haskins, "A Timely Leader," *Cobblestone*; Marcia Amidon Lusted, "Coretta Scott King," *Cobblestone*.

All articles © by Carus Publishing Company. Reproduced with permission.

All Cricket Media material is copyrighted by Carus Publishing Company, d/b/a Cricket Media, and/or various authors and illustrators. Any commercial use or distribution of material without permission is strictly prohibited. Please visit http://www.cricketmedia.com/info/licensing2 for licensing and http://www.cricketmedia.com for subscriptions.

CONTENTS

CHAPTER ONE
SOWING THE SEEDS FOR
THE CIVIL RIGHTS MOVEMENT 4

CHAPTER TWO
FOUR LEADERS FOR FREEDOM 8

CHAPTER THREE
THE CRISIS IS BORN 15

CHAPTER FOUR
ORGANIZING FOR THE CAUSE 20

CHAPTER FIVE
THE FEARLESS IDA B. WELLS-BARNETT . . 25

CHAPTER SIX
CHARLES HAMILTON HOUSTON:
LEARNING FROM THE BEST 32

CHAPTER SEVEN
DR. MARTIN LUTHER KING JR.:
A TIMELY LEADER. 39

GLOSSARY 46
FURTHER READING. 47
INDEX 48

CHAPTER ONE

SOWING THE SEEDS FOR THE CIVIL RIGHTS MOVEMENT

What are civil rights? Civil rights are the rights that all citizens are supposed to have: for example, the right to go to school, to ride a bus, and to eat in a restaurant. The right to vote. The right to be protected equally by the law. But in the United States, the laws have not always been fair. Even after the Civil War ended slavery, black Americans were not treated the same as whites. Many states—particularly in the South—had laws and traditions that discriminated against black Americans. Along with many whites, black citizens have fought against those practices ever since.

JIM CROW PLAGUES THE SOUTH

Following the Civil War, blacks living in the South were segregated from whites on trains and buses, in schools and restaurants, and even in public bathrooms. Some laws made it illegal for blacks and whites to shake hands or play checkers. These racist "Jim Crow laws" got their unusual name from minstrel stage shows. Minstrel shows featured white performers with their faces painted black. The actors were pretending to be African Americans. They portrayed blacks as being inferior whites. One minstrel performer sang a song called "Jump Jim Crow." This song was so popular that the term Jim Crow became a nasty way to refer to black Americans.

African American people were not allowed to use the same drinking fountains as white people.

A Louisiana law said that railroads had to provide "equal but separate accommodations for the white and colored races." In 1892, a light-skinned black man challenged it. Homer Plessey sat in a "whites only" train car. When he told the conductor he was part African American, he was ordered to move. Mr. Plessey refused. He was arrested and convicted of breaking the law. His lawyers fought back. Sadly—shockingly—in a case called *Plessey v. Ferguson*, the US Supreme Court decided that "separate but equal" laws were legal.

Understandably, black—and many white—Americans felt that "separate but equal" laws were terrible. Prejudice and racial problems were becoming worse. In 1908, in Springfield, Illinois, two black men were accused of committing crimes against whites. The arrests triggered race riots. For two long days, whites attacked blacks. They killed two people, injured hundreds, and burned down many black-owned homes and businesses.

THE NAACP RISES TO FIGHT INEQUALITY

After the riots, sixty people met in New York City to discuss the mistreatment of African Americans. Seven were black. The rest were white. (Many white northerners did not support segregation laws or legal discrimination.) This group formed an organization called the National Association for the Advancement of Colored People (NAACP). In 1909 the NAACP began fighting for equal rights for all races.

Forty-one years later, the NAACP was called upon to help fight school segregation. All over the South, schools for black children were in terrible condition. The good schools were reserved for whites. In Topeka, Kansas, thirteen black families tried to enroll their children in white schools. They were turned away.

At about the same time, Barbara Johns was a sixteen-year-old high school student in Virginia. The school she attended was terribly overcrowded. Some of her classes were taught in buses or cold, leaky shacks. The students' school supplies were torn and tattered. Fed up with these terrible conditions, Barbara organized a student strike. Students walked out of school and refused to return until a new school was built. The NAACP wanted to help the students. But the lawyers understood that building a new school for blacks would not solve the real problem of segregation. It would simply continue to follow the racist "separate but equal" laws.

So the NAACP agreed to help the students on one condition: that they give up their demands for a new school and join the bigger fight to end school segregation. Barbara and her fellow

Attorneys George E. C. Hayes (*left*), Thurgood Marshall (*center*), and James Nabrit Jr. smile in front of the US Supreme Court Building after winning the *Brown v. Board of Education* case, which ended segregation in public schools.

students agreed. In 1951, the fight began. Officially known as *Brown v. Board of Education*, the fight involved cases in five places: Barbara Johns and the students in Virginia, the thirteen families in Kansas, plus Delaware, South Carolina, and Washington, DC. After a long fight, history was made. In 1954, the US Supreme Court ruled that school segregation was against the Constitution. "Separate but equal" was no longer legal.

Brown v. Board of Education opened a door for African Americans. But through this door, many more years of struggle were waiting.

views on slavery. Whatever the cause of his death, Walker's words and spirit lived on in his powerful *Appeal*.

NAT TURNER AND HIS REBELLION

It is not known whether the Virginia slave Nat Turner ever saw *Walker's Appeal*. If he had, he probably would have read it, for Turner could read even though it was against Virginia law for slaves to be taught to read.

Nat Turner was born in 1800. His father fled north to be free when Turner was still young. Turner grew up under the care of his mother and grandmother. The two women taught him that he was not meant to be only a slave and that his ability to read was an indication that he had a special mission in life.

What the mission was remained unknown until 1825 when Turner felt he had a vision from God. The vision convinced Turner that there would be an uprising of black slaves against their white masters. "I saw white spirits and black spirits engaged in battle," Turner recalled.

Three years later, he had an even more powerful vision. "I heard a loud voice in the heavens, and the Spirit instantly appeared to me and said … I should arise and prepare myself, and slay my enemies with their own weapons … for the time was fast approaching when the first should be the last and the last should be first."

Turner's rebellion began on August 22, 1831. Armed with hatchets and axes, Turner and his companions entered his master's house and killed all of the inhabitants. Turner then moved on, gathering more men to his cause. At one point, Turner's freedom fighters included more than sixty slaves and free men, and they killed a total of sixty white people.

Within a day, the rebellion had been put down. Some of the rebels had been captured. Other rebels, along with a number of blacks not

Nat Turner and some companions conspire in the woods, planning the rebellion.

involved with the uprising, were killed. Turner alone escaped capture. He hid for two months before being caught, put on trial, and hanged. He went bravely to his death, still believing his actions had been proper.

SOJOURNER TRUTH AND HER LECTURES

Sojourner Truth was truly a traveler on the road to freedom, walking and riding thousands of miles, spreading her message of liberty and equality. Born around 1797 in New York State as Isabella, a black slave, she gained her freedom in 1827. She then turned her tremendous energies toward winning emancipation for all black people. One of her monumental accomplishments was gaining freedom for her son who had been illegally sold into slavery in the South. Her legal victory was a rare case of a black's rights being upheld in a court against the claims of a white.

When she was close to forty years old, Isabella began a journey which was to carry her throughout the North, the South, and the expanding West. Early on this journey she changed her name to Sojourner Truth, to mean a traveler for truth. She traveled from town

to town, speaking at anti-slavery meetings. She argued that no man, woman, or child should ever be enslaved. Her moving speeches captivated and inspired audiences. "I can't read a book, but I can read the people," she was fond of saying.

Just as she delighted some people, Truth infuriated

Sojourner Truth worked hard to gain equal rights for all people.

others. A man once told her that he did not care about her speeches any more than he cared about a flea bite. She replied, "Maybe not, but the Lord willing, I'll keep you scratchin'."

At the end of the Civil War, Truth struggled to get the government to assist the ex-slaves who were rebuilding their lives as free people. Then in her seventies, she was still, in the words of a friend, "teaching, preaching, nursing, watching, and praying" for her people.

Sojourner Truth died in 1883. She was active to the end of her days in the fight for equal rights for blacks and for women as well.

MALCOLM X AND HIS SPEECHES

According to federal law, slavery and inequality ended in the years during and soon after the Civil War. In reality, however, blacks continued to suffer inequality long after the Union and Confederacy were reunited. In many ways, blacks had fewer opportunities than whites and continued to live in a kind of bondage. In the 1960s, the charismatic black leader, Malcolm X, would make a great effort to break these "invisible chains."

Malcolm X, born Malcolm Little in 1925, grew up in Detroit, Michigan. His father, a minister, instilled in him a strict sense of discipline and courage. While Malcolm was still young, his father was killed by a white man.

Although he did well in school, Malcolm Little quit in the eighth grade and moved to Boston, and later to New York. He became involved in drugs, gambling, and robbery, and these crimes led to a prison sentence.

Although not everyone approved of his message or methods, Malcolm X was extremely influential in the struggle for civil rights.

While in prison, Malcolm discovered the Nation of Islam, a black religious group. Upon his release, Malcolm Little became an active member of the Nation. Dropping the name Little because it had been given to his family by their original slave masters, he changed his name to Malcolm X, the X signifying his unknown black ancestry. Malcolm X now put his energies and intelligence into spreading the message of black pride, separation from white America, and the Muslim religion.

In 1964 ,Malcolm X made a pilgrimage to Mecca, Saudi Arabia, the Muslim holy city. There he witnessed the full brotherhood of people of different skin colors. When he returned to America to continue his battle for black rights, he began to speak out in favor of a society where blacks and whites could live together in harmony. He made it clear, however, that if changes were not made peacefully, violence would be necessary.

On February 21, 1965, Malcolm X was assassinated. Through the example of his life and the power of his words, Malcolm X offered the hope that someday, black Americans would gain full equality.

CHAPTER THREE

THE CRISIS IS BORN

I n 1910, W. E. B. Du Bois was trying to figure out how best to reach the largest number of African American citizens. He was in charge of publicity and research for the NAACP. The NAACP, Du Bois thought, needed an official publication that would illustrate "those facts and arguments which show the danger of race prejudice." A monthly magazine called *The Crisis* was born.

REACHING THE MASSES

From the outset, Du Bois acted as the magazine's editor in chief. He controlled the content and tone of the new journal. (This was remarkable because white liberals dominated the leadership of the NAACP's board of directors.) Du Bois intended *The Crisis* to report on current events. He also planned to offer analysis of the news, reviews of literature, and editorials that emphasized "the rights of men."

The Crisis, therefore, covered a wide array of topics. Articles ranged from politics, economics, and education to literature, music, and health. Monthly features included profiles of prominent

W. E. B. Du Bois founded *The Crisis*, the official publication of the NAACP, which aimed to educate the public on the struggle of African Americans for equal rights.

African Americans, a column of recommended books, and directories listing educational and legal services for black people.

One way in which the board of directors insisted that Du Bois show restraint was not to criticize his chief opponent, Booker T. Washington. The board held to this position despite Washington's repeated attacks on the organization and numerous attempts to silence the journal. But Du Bois recognized that the NAACP and its publication could be used to chip away at Washington's perceived position as the leader of black Americans.

Du Bois ordered one thousand copies of the initial edition of *The Crisis* to be printed in November 1910. He believed that the magazine would reach a limited audience. Du Bois miscalculated badly. *The Crisis* struck a chord with men and women from all walks of life, including liberal white and poor black people.

By its second year, *The Crisis* had a circulation of sixteen thousand. By the 1920s, its circulation had reached more than one hundred thousand. The tone of *The Crisis* had a special appeal to African Americans. In one issue, for example, black readers were encouraged to arm themselves against racist assaults. "If we are to die," Du Bois wrote, "in God's name let us perish like men and not like bales of hay." Du Bois also felt that the American government should champion civil rights. To encourage the federal government to act, he made a point of regularly publishing statistics on the number of African Americans lynched in the United States.

African Americans themselves, though, could not entirely avoid Du Bois's criticism. Du Bois scolded many black writers for reinforcing white stereotypes of African Americans as primitives, criminals, or victims.

A RADICAL TURN

Du Bois's sharp criticisms of American race relations began to annoy and frighten some members of the NAACP's board. Their appeals had no influence on Du Bois's editorial policies, however. He had a growing interest in Pan-Africanism. He began to

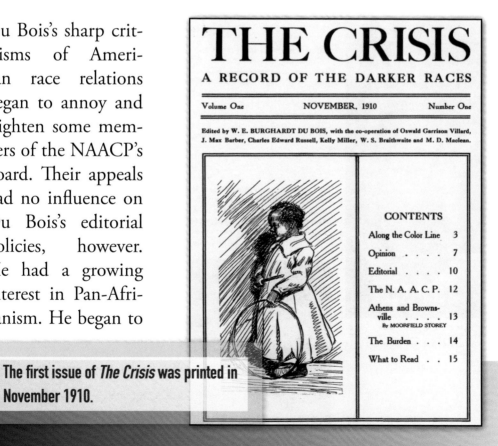

The first issue of *The Crisis* was printed in November 1910.

call for "voluntary segregation" to escape what he saw as unyielding white racism. Du Bois's vocal stand on these issues did nothing to calm the fears or win the favor of the NAACP board.

By the 1930s, Du Bois's growing radicalism prompted the board of directors to issue an ultimatum. If Du Bois did not take back his recent criticisms of the American government and race relations, he would have to resign. It did not take him long to come to a decision.

On May 21, 1934, Du Bois stepped down as editor of *The Crisis* after twenty-four years. He regretted abandoning the magazine to those whom he thought did not have "the ability or the disposition to guide it in the right direction."

Still, whatever differences had arisen between them, the leadership of the NAACP recognized Du Bois's efforts and accomplishments. "He created, what never existed before," reflected one NAACP official, "a Negro intelligentsia, and many who have never read a word of his writings are his spiritual disciples and descendants."

"I HAVE LOVED MY WORK"

His writing efforts for *The Crisis* are just some of the many works that make up W. E. B. Du Bois's legacy. Perhaps his most celebrated book is *The Souls of Black Folk*, published in 1903. The volume is composed of fourteen essays. In them, Du Bois exposed the diversity, tragedy, and promise of African American culture and life.

Du Bois was never reluctant to attempt different types of writing. During his long life, Du Bois's writings included history, sociology, editorials, a biography, two autobiographies, two memoirs, and fiction. The topics of his works include a history of the slave trade

This 1958 photograph shows W. E. B. Du Bois reading in his garden with his wife, Shirley Graham Du Bois, in the background. His wife was also an author and civil rights activist.

and an analysis of black life in Africa and America. He also wrote several works on the concept of race and the problem of racism. And Du Bois completed a study of Africa's role in world affairs. Among his earliest works was *The Philadelphia Negro*, an investigation of the black community in a section of Philadelphia. In 1909, Du Bois published a biography of the abolitionist John Brown. A history of Reconstruction followed in 1935. Two autobiographies, *In Battle for Peace* and *The Autobiography of W. E. B. Du Bois*, detail Du Bois's life.

Du Bois also published five novels. Three of these—*The Ordeal of Mansart, Mansart Builds a School*, and *Worlds of Color*—composed a trilogy titled The Black Flame. These novels focus on the character of Manuel Mansart, a black intellectual coming to grips with racism in America. Many scholars argue that these books mirror Du Bois's own mixed feelings about being a black man in America.

When he died in 1963, Du Bois was at work on the *Encyclopedia Africana,* a massive volume describing African history and culture. Du Bois's farewell, read at his funeral, was one of the most personal pieces of writing he ever produced. In it he said, "I have loved my work, I have loved my people."

CHAPTER FOUR

ORGANIZING FOR THE CAUSE

Over the years, there have a been a number of organizations formed to fight against discriminatory practices experienced by African Americans. These groups range from the Niagara Movement, founded in 1905, to civil rights organizations such as the Black Panther Party, founded in 1966.

THE NIAGARA MOVEMENT

On July 10, 1905, twenty-nine African American men from fourteen states met secretly at a small hotel in Fort Erie, Ontario, Canada, near Niagara Falls. The men discussed the direction their new organization should take. During that first meeting, the group elected W. E. B. Du Bois as its general secretary. As the organizer of the group, Du Bois wanted immediate social and political equality of the races. He encouraged higher education as the key to advancement.

For the second meeting, in Harpers Ferry, West Virginia, in August 1906, Du Bois prepared a stirring speech that stated the goal of the Niagara Movement, as the group called itself. It declared, in

This photo shows the founders of the Niagara Movement.

part, "We claim for our-selves every single right that belongs to a freeborn American, political, civil, and social; and until we get these rights we will never cease to protest and to assail the ears of America."

It was at this gathering that Mary White Ovington met Du Bois. She then wrote about the Niagara Movement for the *New York Evening Post* newspaper. Less than three years later, Ovington and other organizers of the NAACP invited Du Bois to speak at their meeting.

Lack of money prevented the Niagara Movement from really succeeding on a larger national level. But it was able to stage protests, conduct studies on racial prejudice, and initiate lawsuits. As his last act prior to dissolving the movement, Du Bois urged its members to join the newly founded NAACP, with which it shared similar platforms.

THE UNIVERSAL NEGRO IMPROVEMENT ASSOCIATION

Although the NAACP filled a void that many Americans saw in the civil rights movement, there also were other groups that raised their

Marcus Garvey (1887–1940) was a supporter of black nationalism and the Pan–African movement.

voices in the struggle for African American equality. The Universal Negro Improvement Association was founded on the island of Jamaica in 1914 by race activist Marcus Garvey. It greatly appealed to African American pride and nationalism after World War I. The association envisioned a separate African republic where black people would be independent and enjoy self-rule. Garvey's separatist approach, however, clashed with the NAACP. Garvey eventually was expelled to Jamaica by the US government.

THE NATION OF ISLAM

In the 1930s, W. D. Farad began to organize African Americans in Detroit, Michigan. He used Islamic principles to encourage pride and economic independence in his Nation of Islam. In the 1960s, Elijah Muhammad and Malcolm X were two important leaders of the group, which became known as the Black Muslims. Since 1978, Louis Farrakhan has led an offshoot group of the Black Muslims called the Nation of Islam. In October 1995, this organization held its Million Man March in Washington, DC.

CONGRESS OF RACIAL EQUALITY

Founded in 1942, the Congress of Racial Equality's (CORE) strategy was peaceful passive resistance to discrimination. During the 1960s, CORE volunteers and other civil rights workers traveled through the South as "Freedom Riders." Their sit-ins spotlighted discrimination. With one hundred thousand members, CORE remains active today. Its Project Independence is an effective welfare-to-work training program.

Freedom Riders sit beside a burned out bus in 1961. It was burned by an angry mob who attacked the riders on the highway.

THE SOUTHERN CHRISTIAN LEADERSHIP CONFERENCE

The Southern Christian Leadership Conference (SCLC) was founded by Reverend Martin Luther King Jr., Reverend Ralph David Abernathy, and others in 1957. This group coordinated peaceful civil rights activities in the South. Today the SCLC is headed by one of King's sons, Martin Luther King III.

THE STUDENT NON-VIOLENT COORDINATING COMMITTEE

College students in Raleigh, North Carolina, started the Student Non-Violent Coordinating Committee (SNCC) in 1960. Besides joining CORE's Freedom Riders, the group held its own vocal protests and helped African Americans register to vote. Later in the 1960s, SNCC leader Stokely Carmichael stressed Black Power.

THE BLACK PANTHERS

"All Power to All the People!" was the cry of the Black Panthers. Huey Newton and Bobby Seale founded the group in Oakland, California, in 1966 to counter what they considered brutal police treatment of African Americans. Guided by Marxist philosophy, the leaders favored revolution, if necessary, to change society. The Black Panthers had several violent confrontations with police, but they also were involved in peaceful activities such as the establishment of a free breakfast program for children.

CHAPTER FIVE

THE FEARLESS IDA B. WELLS-BARNETT

da B. Wells-Barnett was born into slavery in 1862 in Holly Springs, Mississippi. She became a school teacher, but when a conductor tried to forcibly remove her from a train after she refused to move to the smoking car, her career path took a different turn. She blasted her way through fights on issues with which no one else wanted to get involved. She participated in battles knowing she would lose. A strict sense of justice tempered Wells-Barnett's anger, but her outspokenness and uncompromising nature at times intimidated people. Wells-Barnett and her husband were popular in Chicago. At the turn of the twentieth century, the city had become a center for people known as anti-Bookerites, who were against Booker T. Washington and his viewpoints. To Wells-Barnett and other black leaders, Washington's compromising and accommodating attitude in the fight for African American rights was unacceptable. As Washington gained a more prominent position in the Republican party, the Barnetts gradually lost their influential role. Then, in 1908, the Barnetts openly opposed presidential candidate William Howard Taft, Washington's political ally.

Ida B. Wells–Barnett was known not only for her work for the civil rights movement but also for her work on behalf of women's rights and getting women the right to vote.

WELLS-BARNETT AND THE NAACP

W. E. B. Du Bois also resisted Washington's political philosophy. When Du Bois's controversial book, *The Souls of Black Folk*, was published in 1903, Wells-Barnett hosted a discussion of it in her home, inviting both African Americans and whites. The two African American activist leaders met on several occasions. But their friendship and shared philosophies soon took separate paths.

At the end of the first decade of the 1900s, a group of whites and African Americans were trying to establish the NAACP to challenge Washington's leadership and influence and encourage African Americans to fight actively for their economic, political, and social equality. Critical to the group's success was the Committee of Forty, its interim governing body, which would "determine the ideological mold of the new civil rights organization, choose its board of directors, and hire its staff."

When the NAACP came into existence in 1909, Wells-Barnett and other anti-Bookerites were excluded from the Committee of Forty. Wells-Barnett refused Du Bois's attempts to have her placed on the committee after the fact, but later regretted her decision.

Wells-Barnett turned her energy instead toward denouncing racism. In 1911, she led a delegation to Chicago's city hall in an attempt to prohibit the showing of a racist play by Thomas Dixon Jr. The delegation failed. Then in the spring of 1913, when Oswald Garrison Villard, chairman of the Committee of Forty, convened a meeting of the Chicago branch of the NAACP without informing her, Wells-Barnett withdrew from the association.

Two years later, a movie based on Dixon's novel and play provoked outrage from African Americans nationwide. *Birth of a Nation* portrayed black people in an unflattering light following the Civil War. Considered a film masterpiece and praised by President Woodrow Wilson, it glorified the Ku Klux Klan, an extremist organization that used violence against African Americans, Jews, immigrants, and other groups of people.

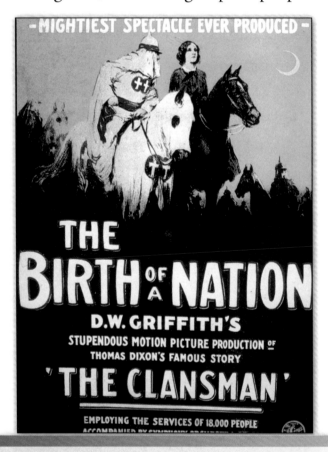

African Americans blocked the movie's presentation in some cities, but they did not block it in Chicago. Wells-Barnett charged that the NAACP had not done enough to protest the offensive film's release. The NAACP claimed it had taken the lead in action against the movie.

This movie poster shows a Ku Klux Klan member as one of the main characters in *The Birth of a Nation*.

FIGHTING INJUSTICE ON ALL FRONTS

Wells-Barnett continued her crusades for justice independent of the NAACP. She became active in suffrage for women and African Americans. Founding the first black women's suffrage group, the Alpha Suffrage Club, Wells-Barnett later expanded it into a protest and self-help organization.

Wells-Barnett campaigned successfully against the passage of a law segregating public transportation in Illinois. She fought bills in Congress that prohibited interracial marriages. In 1915, she attacked segregated social activities at Chicago's integrated Wendell Phillips High School. Wells-Barnett began a letter-writing campaign against a proposed immigration law that would have excluded Africans. She joined with Chicago social worker Jane Addams and others to celebrate the fiftieth anniversary of the Emancipation Proclamation. Her letters to the editors of African American and white newspapers challenged readers to confront bigotry and end discrimination.

Then, during the summer of 1919, economic and social changes swept the nation. World War I had just ended. Race riots occurred in twenty-six American cities. Chicagoans demonstrated for days after it was claimed that a black teenager was stoned to death on a Lake Michigan beach. Thirty-eight people died—most of them African American—and one thousand black and white people were left homeless.

In Arkansas, African American sharecroppers at a union meeting exchanged gunfire with occupants of a passing car. After four

During the Chicago Race Riot of 1919, the police rounded up African American people and brought them to a safe zone.

days of mayhem, hundreds of black men were arrested and put in jail. Twelve of them were sentenced to death in the electric chair.

Wells-Barnett received a letter from one of the accused. She traveled to Arkansas, where she met with the prisoners' families. Wells-Barnett went with them to the jail, passing herself off as a relative. "Dying is the last thing you ought to even think about, much less talk about. Pray to live and believe you are going to get out," she advised them.

Wells-Barnett and the NAACP mirrored each other's efforts. She printed her findings in a pamphlet; NAACP staffer and future secretary Walter White published newspaper articles across the country. All the condemned men were released by January 1925. When NAACP leaders claimed the credit for saving the men and did not offer Wells-Barnett any credit for her work, her relationship with the group worsened.

Concerned about growing indifference toward civil rights, in 1930, sixty-eight-year-old Wells-Barnett made a run for a state senate seat in Illinois. She received only 585 votes, but she continued to work and write.

A year after recovering from gallbladder surgery, Wells-Barnett died of uremic poisoning in 1931. By that time, she had been nearly forgotten by those who were benefiting from her passion for justice. The woman who had exasperated colleagues and critics enjoyed more prestige after her death than during her lifetime. Her radical stance in the fight for civil rights earned Ida B. Wells-Barnett her contemporaries' dismay and a place in the history books.

CHAPTER SIX

CHARLES HAMILTON HOUSTON: LEARNING FROM THE BEST

Charles Hamilton Houston was perhaps the most important influence on African American lawyers who came of age in the 1930s and 1940s and on the mid-twentieth-century legal crusade against racial discrimination.

Born in 1895, Houston grew up in Washington, DC, where he attended the city's segregated schools, including its excellent M Street High School, the region's finest classical school for black children. Houston enrolled at the largely white Amherst College in Massachusetts (he was the only black student in the class of 1915), graduating with honors. After briefly teaching English at Howard University in Washington, Houston enlisted in the army as the United States entered World War I.

The military was a highly segregated institution. Black soldiers were often treated harshly and commanded by unsympathetic whites. Houston entered the only all-black officer-training program, at Fort Des Moines in Iowa, was promoted to first lieutenant, and eventually served in the American Expeditionary Force in Europe. Outraged by the unjust and racist treatment of black soldiers, Houston concluded that he would "never get caught … without

Charles Houston was the chief counsel for the NAACP from 1935 until 1940.

knowing something about my rights; that if luck was with me, and I got through this war, I would study law and use my time fighting for men who could not strike back."

Houston survived the war and carried out his promise to himself. Following in the footsteps of his father, who was a prominent attorney in Washington, Houston enrolled at Harvard University Law School from 1919 to 1923. From 1924 to 1929, he joined his father's

Howard University was founded in 1867 to allow African Americans to receive a high-quality college education.

law firm, now called "Houston and Houston." In 1929, however, he made a momentous decision that would have important implications for the future of the civil rights struggle: at the age of thirty-four, he became vice-dean of Howard University Law School.

TRAINING "SOCIAL ENGINEERS"

In his six years in that position, he transformed Howard into the nation's finest African American law school, improving its educational standards and attracting excellent faculty members and students.

Houston's efforts involved more than making Howard's law school an excellent educational institution. Houston also transformed it into a dynamic force for legal and social change. He believed that the law school should train African American students not only to know the law but to use the law to challenge discrimination and racial inequality. Black law students, he believed, should become "sentinels guarding against wrong." The black lawyer, Houston argued, "must be trained as a social engineer and group interpreter. Due to the Negro's social and political condition … the Negro lawyer must be prepared to anticipate, guide, and interpret his group advancement."

Thurgood Marshall, who attended Howard Law School from 1930 to 1933 and studied under Houston, recalled that the Howard dean "insisted that we get out into the field and become 'social engineers' and not just lawyers. You had to be as good [as] if not better than the white lawyer in order to win, and he wanted the Negro lawyers to make a contribution to the overall picture of the country."

Charles Houston makes a plea for the equal use of the Central High auditorium in 1939.

ENDING SEGREGATION IN EDUCATION

Charles Houston practiced what he preached. Not content to oversee the law school and train a new generation of black lawyers, he dedicated himself to using the law to bring about social change and racial equality. In 1935, he left Howard to become "special counsel" in charge of the legal program of the NAACP. His main target was "separate but equal" education for African American students.

Houston put forth a long-term strategy to undermine segregation in education. He did so first by using the law to force white officials to spend more money to provide "equal" facilities. Then, he used the law to declare such segregation unconstitutional, because there could be "no true equality under a segregated system." Houston's campaign, on which Marshall worked extensively, produced significant victories.

In the *Murray v. The University of Maryland* case, a Maryland court ordered the university to admit Donald Murray, a black student, to the law school instead of giving him a scholarship to study out of state. In *Gaines v. Canada*, the US Supreme Court declared that the University of Missouri, as a taxpayer-funded state school, could not deny Lloyd Gaines admission on the grounds of his race. Eventually, the NAACP's campaign against segregated educational facilities would result in the historic *Brown v. Board of Education* case in 1954.

THE TRIUMPHS CONTINUE

Returning to private practice in 1938, Houston continued to work with Marshall and other NAACP attorneys and accepted new cases dealing with racial discrimination in employment. From the late 1930s until 1950, Houston actively represented groups of African American railroad workers in the South who were excluded from white unions and subject to unequal treatment on the job.

In 1943, he served as a lawyer for the US government's Fair Employment Practices Committee, presenting its case against racist white railroad unions and managers. In 1944, Houston won two major cases before the US Supreme Court. Both ruled that white railroad unions could not negotiate contracts with employers who discriminated against black railroaders. In 1948, he won an important victory against discrimination in housing before the Supreme Court in *Shelley v. Kraemer*, which ruled that legal documents forbidding the sale or rental of property to African Americans (known as "restrictive covenants") were unconstitutional.

Houston died of heart disease in April 1950 at the age of fifty-four. At his funeral in Washington, his friend, William H. Hastie, a federal judge, declared Houston to be a "Moses" who guided African Americans "through the wilderness of second-class citizenship" and who lived "to see us close to the promised land of full equality under the law."

CHAPTER SEVEN

DR. MARTIN LUTHER KING JR.: A TIMELY LEADER

D r. Martin Luther King Jr. was the right man at the right time. African American leaders before him, such as W. E. B. Du Bois, Mary McLeod Bethune, and A. Philip Randolph, had possessed some of the same qualities, and African Americans had had other opportunities to win their civil rights. But during the 1950s and 1960s, a combination of events made American society open to change, and the young Baptist minister who was thrust into the headlines as a result of the 1955–1956 Montgomery, Alabama, bus boycott had the moral conviction and ability to inspire that were needed to bring about that change.

POWERED BY PEACE

King, the son of a minister who had been born in 1929 in Atlanta, Georgia, did not seek a leadership role in the bus boycott and was reluctant at first to accept election as president of the Montgomery Improvement Association, which was formed to publicize and raise money to support the boycott. But he

Martin Luther King Jr. is perhaps the most well-known civil rights activist in history, particularly for promoting peaceful protests rather than acts of violence.

was excited about the opportunity to put into practice the principles of nonviolent protest that Mohandas "Mahatma" Gandhi had used successfully to help win India's independence from Great Britain in the 1940s. King had dreamed about the possibility of using Gandhi's "soul force" to attack the problem of racial segregation in the United States.

At the time, the church was the center of the African American community, and it was no accident that black ministers were in the forefront of the civil rights movement. King stood out among black Baptist ministers not only for his brilliance as an orator but also for his strong belief that Americans had a basic sense of decency that would respond to nonviolent protests and the sheer force of moral right. He also had the ability to inspire others to follow him and, when the civil rights movement became more confrontational, to grow as a leader.

THE RIGHT ENVIRONMENT FOR JUSTICE

But even a black Baptist minister as special as King could well have been merely a voice in the wilderness had it not been for the convergence of events. World War II had caused people around the world to think seriously about basic human rights and the tragedy that could result from one group's hatred of another. It was difficult for some white Americans to justify the segregation of blacks in their society during the postwar era, and it was difficult for blacks who had fought in the US Armed Forces to return home and be subjected to second-class citizenship.

Change had already begun in the late 1940s, with President Harry S. Truman's executive order banning segregation in the armed forces. It continued in the early 1950s when, after a long and carefully planned campaign in the nation's courts, attorneys for the NAACP won *Brown v. Board of Education*. Although the landmark US Supreme Court ruling declared only segregated education unconstitutional, Americans, both white and black, realized that the implications of the decision extended into every area of society.

Finally, advances in technology made the time right for mass protest. When southern whites responded to civil rights protests with violence, television broadcast the stark and ugly images across the nation and around the world. It was impossible for Americans to ignore what was going on—and impossible for local officials to portray the incidents as isolated events.

Martin Luther King Jr. could speak to a television camera as effectively as he could to a church congregation, and the media played a major role in creating his image as a moral leader of the nation. Thousands of people—black and white, young and old, educated and uneducated—responded to his call and risked losing their jobs, their homes, and their lives in the civil rights struggle. They looked to him as a beacon of hope and inspiration. The international community recognized his importance by awarding him the Nobel Peace Prize in 1964.

Once the framework for guaranteeing civil rights had been laid by the Civil Rights Act of 1964 and the Voting Rights Act of 1965, King turned his attention to Vietnam and spoke out against US involvement in what he believed was a civil war. He was widely criticized for this stance, even by supporters of the civil rights movement.

It is not clear whether King would have been able to wield the same power in other causes as he had in civil rights. He was assassinated in 1968. But the influence he exerted during this crucial time in the nation's history has been recognized by the adoption of a national holiday commemorating his birthday. King is the only non-president in US history to be so honored.

Martin Luther King Jr. gave moving speeches that inspired action in his listeners. Here he speaks to the large crowd at the 1963 March on Washington. It was during this demonstration that King delivered his historic "I Have a Dream" speech.

CORETTA SCOTT KING

Coretta Scott's marriage to the Reverend Dr. Martin Luther King Jr. in 1953 resulted in a very public role for her in the modern civil rights movement. But her commitment to social justice and peace existed both before and extended after her married life with King.

Coretta Scott was born on April 27, 1927, in Marion, Alabama. She graduated valedictorian from her high school in 1945 and earned bachelor's degrees in music and education from Antioch College in Yellow Springs, Ohio. She later transferred to the New England Conservatory of Music in Boston, where she studied singing and violin. While in Boston, a friend introduced her to Martin Luther King who was working on his doctorate in systematic theology at Boston University. Like many activists, Scott's personal experience with discrimination prompted her to join the NAACP and the Race Relations and Civil Liberties committees in college.

A year after the Kings moved to Montgomery, Alabama, in 1954, the Montgomery Bus Boycott began. King was asked to lead it. Coretta Scott King later acknowledged that she sensed that her husband was becoming part of a historic movement. She worked for the cause—speaking, traveling, and marching with her husband—while also raising four children.

After her husband's assassination in 1968, Coretta Scott King stepped in as the leader of the civil rights movement. She established the Martin Luther King Jr. Center for Nonviolent Social Change in Atlanta, Georgia. The center has helped train tens of thousands of people in King's pacifist methods. She also led the campaign to make her husband's birthday a national holiday. She used her influence to

Coretta Scott King speaks at the 1988 Democratic National Convention in Atlanta, Georgia. She was an activist for several different causes throughout her life.

be a vocal and powerful advocate for civil and human rights not only for African Americans, but for women, children, the gay and lesbian community, and the poor and homeless as well. She also championed religious freedom, health care, education, nuclear disarmament, and environmental justice. Coretta Scott King died on January 30, 2006, at the age of seventy-eight.

GLOSSARY

bigotry Intolerance of another's religion, race, or politics.

discrimination Unjust or unfair treatment of people, especially in relation to race, gender, or religion.

intelligentsia The intellectually superior group in a society.

interim Temporary.

Islamic principles Ways of believing or behaving that include acceptance of and submission to God and Mohammed as the last prophet of God.

Marxist philosophy The ideals of Karl Marx and Communism, which advocates the overthrow of a capitalist (business-driven) government by the working-class people.

prejudice An opinion or judgment about a person—or a whole group of people—that is not based on facts or knowledge.

prestige A person's high standing among others.

racism The belief that some people are inferior to others simply because they are of a different race.

segregate To separate people by enforcing unfair laws that keep them apart.

separatist A person who advocates disassociation from a group or political unit.

sharecropper A farmer who works for a share of the crops he or she raises on land owned by others.

sit-in A demonstrations in which protesters passively sit in a restaurant, waiting room, or other public facility until they are either served or physically removed.

ultimatum A statement that implies the threat of serious penalties if certain terms are not accepted.

uremic poisoning A condition of the kidneys resulting from waste product retention in the bloodstream.

BOOKS

Bernard, Catherine. *Sojourner Truth: Women's Rights Activist and Abolitionist.* New York, NY: Enslow Publishing, 2016.

Burlingame, Jeff. *Malcolm X: Fighting for Human Rights.* New York, NY: Enslow Publishing, 2017.

Cunningham, Meghan M. Engsberg. *W. E. B. DuBois: Co-Founder of the NAACP.* New York, NY: Cavendish Square Publishing, 2017.

Morretta, Alison. *Ida B. Wells-Barnett and the Crusade Against Lynching.* New York, NY: Cavendish Square Publishing, 2016.

Schuman, Michael A., and Anne E. Schraff. *Martin Luther King Jr.: Fighting for Civil Rights.* New York, NY: Enslow Publishing, 2017.

Torres, John A., and Sarah Betsy Fuller. *Desegregating Schools: Brown v. Board of Education.* New York, NY: Enslow Publishing, 2017.

WEBSITES

BlackPast.org

blackpast.org

An online guide to African American history, including "101 African American Firsts," primary documents, major speeches, and historical timelines.

PBS, Civil Rights Icons

pbs.org/black-culture/explore/civil-rights-leaders/#.WQemclKZMkg

Facts and footage of interviews with some of the most influential leaders in the civil rights movement.

INDEX

A

Alpha Suffrage Club, 29

B

Birth of a Nation, 27–28
Black Panthers, 20, 24
Brown v. Board of Education,
   7, 37, 42

C

Carmichael, Stokely, 24
Civil War, 4, 13, 28
Congress of Racial Equality
   (CORE), 23, 24
Crisis, The, 15–18

D

Du Bois, W. E. B., 15–19,
   20–21, 27, 39

F

Farad, W. D., 22
Farrakhan, Louis, 22–23
Freedom Riders, 23, 24

G

Gaines, Lloyd, 37
Gandhi, Mohandas
   "Mahatma," 41
Garvey, Marcus, 22

H

Houston, Charles Hamilton,
   32, 34–35, 37–38
Howard University Law
   School, 35, 37

J

Jefferson, Thomas, 8
Jim Crow laws, 4–5
Johns, Barbara, 6–7

K

King, Coretta Scott, 44–45
King, Martin Luther, Jr.,
   24, 39, 41–43, 44
Ku Klux Klan, 28

M

Malcolm X, 13, 14, 22
Marshall, Thurgood, 35,
   37, 38
Million Man March, 23
Montgomery Bus Boycott,
   39, 44
*Murray v. The University of
   Maryland*, 37

N

National Association for
   the Advancement
   of Colored People
   (NAACP), 6, 15–18,
   21–22, 27, 28, 29, 31,
   37, 38, 42, 44
Nation of Islam, 14, 22–23
Niagara Movement, 20–21
Nobel Peace Prize, 42

O

Ovington, Mary White, 20

P

Plessey v. Ferguson, 5
Plessey, Homer, 5

R

race riots, 5, 29

S

Shelly v. Kraemer, 38
Southern Christian Lead-
   ership Conference
   (SCLC), 24
Student Non-Violent
   Coordinating
   Committee (SNCC),
   24

T

Truth, Sojourner, 11–13
Turner, Nat, 10–11

U

Universal Negro Improve-
   ment Association,
   21–22

W

Walker, David, 8–10
Walker's Appeal, 9–10
Washington, Booker T., 16,
   25, 27
Wells-Barnett, Ida B., 25,
   27–29, 31